be kind to strangers

carl miller daniels

BareBackPress

This is a work of fiction. The characters, incidents, and dialogue are the products of the author's imagination and are not to be construed as real. Any resemblance to actual events or person, living or dead, is entirely coincidental.

BareBackPress
Hamilton, Ontario, Canada
For enquires visit www.barebackpress.com
For information contact press@barebacklit.com
Cover layout by Choi Yunnam
Cover photography by Carl Miller Daniels

No part of this can be used or reproduced in any manner whatsoever without written permission, except in the case of brief quotations embodied in critical articles and reviews. For information address BareBackPress.

COPYRIGHT © 2015 Carl Miller Daniels
All RIGHTS RESERVED
ISBN-13: 978-1926449043
ISBN-10: 1926449045

POEMS

be kind to strangers 9

the innocence of atlantic sledgehammers 11

twisted hair 12

peripheral satellite cop 13

flavor 16

homesick pajamas 17

the hopscotch of philosophy 18

surgery 20

picking daisies 21

gurgle 23

propane 25

nuts & bolts & ginger snaps 27

now now diurnal tryptophan 28

one-two buckle my shoe 30

blowing out the candle 33

green 35

birthstone 36

pony farm 38

alive 40

the dewberry capital of america 41

the rewards of subtlety 43

better pounce on it 44

plasma pilfering 46

triton the magnificent 48

the good ship lollipop 49

the invincibility clause 50

For Lee Thorn

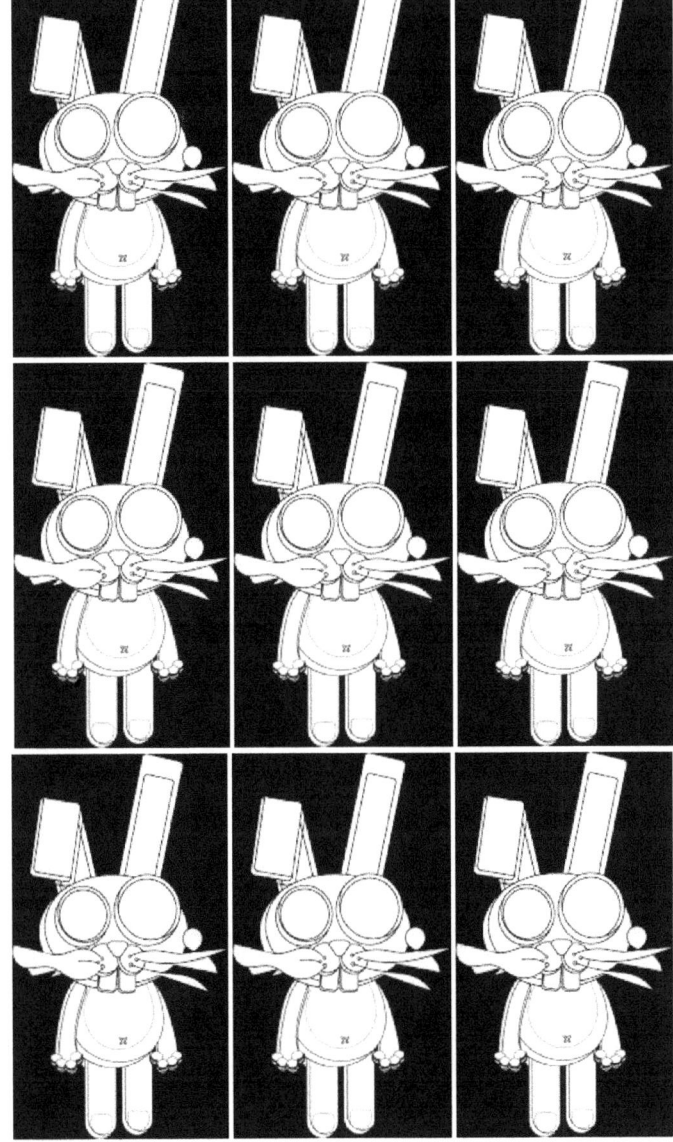

be kind to strangers

evidently my filing system isn't sophisticated enough
to answer these kinds of questions,
but where did adam's very first ejaculation
get spurted?
back before there was eve,
did adam lie there on his back, all hot and sexy
and sexed-up, and did he
tug gently on his big beautiful barely-used-at-all
dick until he spurted cum, and it went
all over his taut sexy chest and belly?
or did adam's very first ejaculation
happen while he was asleep,
while he was having this nebulous
murky kind of dream,
and when he woke up, his big smooth
dick was hard as a rock, and he
was spurting a little geyser of cum
all over himself?
back before there was eve,
i wonder: where DID adam spurt
his cum?
sweet sexy horned-up adam,
all sexed-up and his big dick
turgid and shapely and
just meant for gripping,
just the right shape and
texture, and form,
adam standing there in
the forest
tugging on it gently
and that rush of orgasmo-heat-
pleasure that jolted through
him while his dick
was spurting cum,
was that where the very
first adam ejaculation went?
onto the surface of
the mossy ground in the middle
of the hot sunny woods?

the sun beams on adam's sexy
naked shoulders,
cream-colored droplets on the
tops of his feet.
**
i've checked my filing
system several times,
but it's just not
sophisticated enough
to provide that kind
of information. where
oh where
DID adam spurt his
first blobs of cum? where
did they go? what did
they smell like, all gooey
and musky and male.
adam's nose quivering,
that look of sweet
puzzlement in
his sad sexy eyes.

the innocence of atlantic sledgehammers

tongues of fire in the land of daydreams,
as two sexy naked big-dicked teenage boys
play with each other's big hard dicks
until they both spurt
big gooey globs of cum all over
each other's taut tight firm young bellies.
"ummm," they both say,
as they lick their full pink lips
and watch the goo run down
toward pubic hair
and dick shaft
and tight tender balls.
"i have dreamed of this kind of love,"
says
one of the two sexy naked big-dicked teenage boys.
"and it was precisely this kind of messy," says the other.
and then it's off to
the shower with them,
the slow gentle washing of each other's backs,
watery plumes of
shampoo
bubbles
turning from blue to soft frothy
green.

twisted hair

the man known as Augustus the Good
put pic-nic tables in all the parks,
and as a result was eternally revered, and even
became known as Augustus the God.
**
many years later, when children were advised
of these facts,
they seemed mildly amused, nothing more.
**
even their parents seemed to have forgotten
Augustus the God, and
the significance of all those pic-nic tables.
**
nobody much went on pic-nics anymore, anyway.
**
but big strapping big-dicked boys,
when they hit the age when fucking was really
the only thing on their minds,
sometimes did use the pic-nic tables
for fucking. spread-eagle on these
Augustan tables, they
took turns fucking and
being fucked by each
other, geysers of
cum, orgiastic
ecstasy.
**
well,
that sorta put the zing back into
pic-nic tables.
**
and Augustus, too.
**
as you might
well
imagine.

peripheral satellite cop

the conquistador swing of matador dick,
the punctured bull pumping blood onto the sand,
the white sun blazing in the opalescent
sky -- this is the dream of the
sexy sophomore college boy
as he lies on his back naked in
his bed, his big dick hard as a rock,
lifting his sheet above his
hot flat belly.
**
the roommate who is watching the
sleeping matador dreamer
is wearing
only tight white underpants.
his own big hard dick is sticking out of
the stretched-open fly of
those tight white underpants.
**
the matador dreamer
wakes up,
sees his roommate staring
down at him.
"i thought i told you
to stop doing that,"
says the matador dreamer.
"indeed you did tell me
to stop doing that," says
the roommate.
**
both sexy sophomore boys,
the matador dreamer and
his roommate,
stare into each other's
eyes through softly filtered
light.
**
"so what were you
dreaming about tonight?" says
the roommate to

the sexy sophomore college boy
who had been dreaming about
a sexy big-dicked matador and a
punctured and thrashing
blood-pumping bull.
"nothin," says the matador dreamer.
"that so?" says the roommate.
"yep," says the matador dreamer. "anyways,
i can't remember."
**
they can both smell a lie.
it sticks in the room like the
aroma of hot cum.
**
nobody says anything.
**
then, as they've done before,
in past episodes
of a
similar nature,
they pull the
top sheet off of the matador
dreamer.
the matador dreamer's dick is
still hard, thick,
pulsing.
his roommate starts
masturbating.
the matador dreamer
starts masturbating,
too.
soon, they both spurt cum.
all the cum, both the
roommate's and the
matador dreamer's,
goes right onto the matador
dreamer's taut flat
sexy belly, as if lured there
by the willing texture of
the smooth young flesh.
then, the roommate climbs

into his own bunk,
the top bunk. the
matador dreamer remains in his own
bed on
the bottom. there's a moment
of mutual understanding while the matador
dreamer wipes the cum off
his belly with a soft smooth
towel. soon, both
boys are
are snoring like those big meat saws
in a butcher shop, all primed up and
ready,
to split a carcass in half.

flavor

oh yes, it is indeed possible that Zac Efron is the
sexiest most handsome young man on the planet.
yes, it is indeed possible that every young gay boy,
that every gay teenage boy,
that every gay young man, that every gay 30-something
man, that every gay middle-age man, and that every gay old man
on the planet
who has ever seen even one photograph of Zac Efron or
who has seen Zac Efron act in even one movie
entertains the thought of gently licking
Zac Efron's balls.
and yes,
it is indeed possible that ANYbody on the planet
with any sense knows that
Zac Efron, yes, KNOWS
that Zac Efron is almost excruciatingly attractive,
knows
that Zac Efron is handsome beyond almost
all standard measures of handsomeness,
knows that Zac Efron is
sexy way beyond almost all measures of sexiness.
gay males, straight females, and no doubt
bi males and bi females, too, think
about Zac Efron in terms that are sexual.
some straight males, too, yes males
who know that they are heterosexual, perhaps
nonetheless find themselves thinking
about Zac Efron in terms that are
frankly, sexual. in fact, some heterosexual
males are no doubt disturbed to wake
up in the middle of the night
fresh from a dream involving an imagined Zac Efron
movie and a Zac Efron scene
is which there is full frontal nudity of
a Zac Efron kind.
Most disturbing of all, to these kind
of men, is that whenever they spell
his name, they always spell it
right.

homesick pajamas

the sly fox of a breeder boy just liked to fuck.
he liked the thrust of his hips, the contractions
of his muscles, as he thrust his big smooth hard
dick into the receptacle of the moment.
good god, how this sweet sexy
sly fox of a breeder boy liked to fuck.
the feel of his dick against warmth,
the feel of his butt muscles contracting
and stretching, his belly muscles
contracting and expanding,
as he thrust his big dick into
its appointed target.
ummm.
**
now,
alone in his space ship as it zooms
toward the stars,
he watches little pointy dots of steller debris,
and
questions certain decisions
that he's made in the
last few years,
especially
this one, as the
radio crackles, and
cackles, and sputters
like a puppet, tangled and
lost in
its own gossamer strings.

the hopscotch of philosophy

nowhere are the cattle bigger and more full of milk
than in that barn with the sexy naked big-dicked teenage boy.
oh how he wraps his fingers around their swollen teats
and fills buckets and jars and glasses with
their warm sweet milk. oh how he gives himself
over to absolute pleasure and bends down
and sucks their fresh milk right out of
their warm pink teats. the smell of their
warm hair, the smell of their hide,
the hay, the
crispy corn kernels upon which
they munch and work their jaws as
the sexy naked big-dicked teenage boy is
sitting on a little wooden 3-legged stool
in the sweet hay-smelling barn,
and he is milking all the cows that
are waiting for the loving touch of
his fingers on their teats, the loving
touch of his lips on their teats,
and as he sits there naked
big-dicked and happily horny
on the little 3-legged stool
in the hay-sweet-smelling barn,
he milks the big warm cows and he
drinks their
sweet warm milk
and he feels really really good
as his hot thick dick starts spurting
cum
he's not even touching his dick,
not touching his dick at all, but
he's touching all those teats, instead,
as he sits there on
the little 3-legged stool
the cow he has his hands on
at this moment now has his
freshly-spurted cum dripping
down her hot hairy
flank, and he

swallows, and
blinks, and goes
right on touching her
warm pink teats with
his hot eager fingers.
**
later, at the refrigerator
in the kitchen with
his mom,
he looks at the ice-cold cartons
of milk, but he can't
touch the stuff.
he just can't do it.
can't say what he means,
but if he could, though, it
would be something
about violating the sanctity of
worship, and
defiling the purity
of
joy.
**
"drink yer milk,"
she says.
"or it's gonna be the
paddle on your
sweet little butt."
**
at school that day,
the musky smell
of the other boys
tightens his own
scrotum,
puts a film
on his teeth.

surgery

Bradley Cooper's dick.
Anton Yelchin's dick.
Bradley Cooper's dick in Anton Yelchin's ass.
Anton Yelchin's dick in Bradley Cooper's ass.
**
my own fingers wrapped around my own dick,
my hernia scar fresh, angry-looking, hint
of a bandage still there.
**
Bradley Cooper's dick inserted into Anton Yelchin's mouth.
Anton Yelchin's dick inserted into Bradley Cooper's mouth.
**
my own fingers wrapped around my own dick.
**
my hernia scar still mad.
crazy love.
weird lust and crazy light,
the spring-time clock
busted to daylight saving time,
some mad rush of power,
by those
who got to do
exactly what they thought
they wanted.
**
Anton Yelchin's cum in Bradley Cooper's mouth.
Bradley Cooper's cum in Anton Yelchin's mouth.
**
Bradley Cooper's cum in Anton Yelchin's ass.
Anton Yelchin's cum in Bradley Cooper's ass.
**
hernia surgery was no fun,
but at least, now
i'm fixed.

picking daisies

pacing to the left, then to
the right,
the skinny little art major college boy
practically wore down the carpet
in his room, he paced so much.
the skinny little art major college boy
was totally naked, clothes bothered
him when he was in his worry mode,
and he was sure in his worry mode
now,
ah yes indeed,
he was quite the worrier.
everything worried him.
everything made him fret.
he worried and worried and worried
and fretted and fretted and
paced to the left and
then to the right
and outside it started
to rain and then thunder and
lightning and
then gusts of wind rattled
his bedroom window and still
the skinny naked little art major college boy
went right on
pacing and worrying and fretting.
the level of his anxiety
could be described as a 10 on a
scale of 1 to 10
and when
the rain and thunder and lightning
and wind finally stopped,
the skinny naked little art major college boy
suddenly quit
pacing,
sometimes jerking off really helped
calm him down for a few moments,
he'd seen it work that way before,
more than once, in fact,

and so he
lay down on his back
on top of his bed and
tugged on his surprisingly
big vigorously rock-hard dick for a while
until he spurted cum all
over his skinny naked chest and belly
and then he wiped it off himself
and lay there staring wide-eyed
at the ceiling, and then wouldn't ya know
goddammit this time jerking off
didn't calm him down all that
much now did it
and so then
it was right back to
fretting and worrying and
fretting some more so he
got right back out of bed
and paced some more
and wore down the carpet some more
and
by now it was well after midnight
but still the skinny naked little art major college boy
couldn't sleep,
still he worried and fretted
and worried some more,
it was all just so
fucking much -- he worried
about everything, this,
that, whatever crossed his
mind, he couldn't stop
thinking about it,
this, that, the
other, just EVERYthing --
now take
Edvard Munch's
THE SCREAM, for instance --
one of them
recently sold for 55 million,
now how could anyone
sleep after that?

gurgle

once upon a time, in the deep dark meadow,
there lived a very bad, but very-good-looking young man.
every morning he crawled out of his hole and
went foraging for berries, tubers, fruits, and
slow-moving lizards, all of which he ate
without cleaning them, or even rinsing them, first.
occasionally this very bad, but very-good-looking
young man would happen upon
a lost and careless boy, and he would anally rape
that boy and send that boy butt-ravished and weeping
on his way.
the very bad, but very-good-looking young man
liked nothing more than to happen upon a
sweet, sexy, succulent, and unguardedly clueless boy.
once, when the very bad, but very-good-looking young man
was out foraging for tasty treats in the morning
sun, he happened upon
a group of several boy scouts, all huddled together
in their big ole tan canvas relic of a tent.
he crept in his stealthy way into the tent,
bound and gagged everyone, and had his
way with their tight tender young butts.
then, he ran off into the meadow, howling
with the sexual glow of his rapacious triumph.
trouble soon followed. dogs and men
with guns and planes circling overhead.
the very bad, but very-good-looking young man
stayed hidden in his hole in the meadow
for several days and nights, until
a particularly savvy doggie ran into
the hole and was immediately throttled
and eaten by the very bad, but very-good-looking
young man. then, more
dogs appeared. and more planes
and more police and even more dogs
after that, until, eventually,
the very bad, but very-good-looking young man
was dragged naked kicking spitting
and growling from his hole in

the meadow. after that,
things were never the same again,
there in that meadow.
tubers grew plentiful, as did
berries, and bright shiny lizards.
sometimes boys came there to
play, and when they saw
that empty hole in the ground,
they made some stupid comment
about safety, and respect,
and the land of the lost.
meanwhile, deep within
the walls of an
institute for the criminally
insane, the
very bad, but very-good-looking young man
plans his escape, and
has honed the art of masturbation
into something so beautiful,
that the staff always gathers to watch,
and place bets,
and contemplate the meaning of
it all.

propane

i visited the town of Warm Yogurt, Virginia, where
blood once ran in the streets.
but now, sexy big-dicked young men walk around Warm Yogurt
as if nothing had happened.
they fill out the fronts of their sexy trousers.
they run laps, half-naked, in their flimsy little
paper-thin shorts. when their
dicks get hard, they secret themselves
away in their little secret sex spots of privacy, and
there they tug on their big hard dicks until
they spurt out big gooey globs of
hot musky cum,
and then these sexy big-dicked young men
feel ultra-relaxed for a while,
for a few hours anyway,
until their dicks get hard
again, and once again, these issues must
be re-dressed.
**
oh yes, i often visit the town of Warm Yogurt, Virginia,
where most all of the sadness has pretty much been replaced
by sexy big-dicked young men, and
the smell of their gentle cum is in the
warm mountain air, and
the breath of the nation, is
perfumed with their booze.
**
i like walking
along the side streets of
Warm Yogurt, Virginia, where the big
houses stand; the shrubs and bushes
are trimmed so beautifully,
it makes my skin crawl, but
in a good kind of way. in
reality i do love
those houses, and i do love those side
streets -- in the daytime,
the glint of
the sunshine, and at nighttime,

the smug old face
of that cold
distant moon.

nuts & bolts & ginger snaps

tiny spiderlings covered the branches of the tiny tree,
and leapt into the wind, carried aloft by the
threads of spiderweb they had emitted from their
tiny spiderling butts. soon, all the spiderlings
were as dust among the clouds; some of them
would never descend to earth ever ever again,
and would eventually perish of starvation,
amongst the cold swirling mists. however,
others of them, would descend, and find
a home, and eat a barrel's worth of insects
before their demise.
**
the sexy naked big-dicked teenage boy lay on his
back on his bed and spurted a plume of hot
gooey cum. it plopped onto his sexy naked chest
and onto his sexy naked belly, and clung there,
kind of hot and kind of drippy.
the sexy naked big-dicked teenage boy gave
his big hard dick a couple more gentle tugs--don't
want to tug too hard right after cumming, otherwise
it's painful--anyhow, he gave his nice smooth
big thick dick a couple more gentle tugs,
and then reached over to the table beside
his bed, lifted a soft old t-shirt from
the top, and gently wiped the warm smelly cum
off of his chest and belly.
**
a little spiderling blew into his room
through the open window, and
settled onto his lamp shade, a harmless
presence really,
hardly worth noticing.
the sexy naked big-dicked teenage boy
turned out the lamp,
and went to sleep, as the
little spiderling spun the tiniest
little web imaginable, just a
wee little trifle of a thing, really,
so delicate it was almost cute.

now now diurnal tryptophan

the sexy naked big-dicked teenage boy
stood at the edge of the meadow,
looking down at the little
white flowers that were blooming
profusely in the warm light of the summertime
sun. he was in a great mood.
he felt like giving himself a thousand million
orgasms, one for each and every
flower that was exploding there in front
of him.
**
"god, what a beautiful day. god,
what a wonderful day," thought the
sexy naked big-dicked teenage boy
as he tugged gently on his big smooth massive
dick, hard, and thick, and shiny,
until, very soon, he
watched the cum explode out of its
tip,
savored the moment, savored the
sensation of harsh orgasm and
its gentle nerve-soothing after-effects.
**
now, the sexy naked big-dicked teenage boy
wanted another one, another orgasm,
right now, right this minute, and he
wanted it immediately!
but that was pretty much impossible.
his dick was now soft, and he would
have to wait a while for it to
"re-charge".
but he didn't want to wait
he didn't want to wait
he never ever wanted to wait.
**
his good mood evaporated.
**
it was a beautiful day,
but

way too long,
and all those goddamn little white flowers,
well, they
could just go
fuck themselves.
**
when the earth is a zillion
years old,
how does anyone
go on?
and why do they
do it? with
the hint of summer
fading, and the
breath of winter
feeding on the
curly twists of time.

one-two buckle my shoe

you think any of this makes sense?
that some people bloom and prosper, and
other people wilt and die?
that the fruit punch at a party
for an 18-yr-old sex-god beautiful boy
not only contains alcohol,
but tastes really really good?
that the art created
by a van-gogh wannabee
goes unnoticed and unloved
and finally gets thrown
out with left-over home construction
materials?
you think any of this makes sense?
oh come on now. i suppose
you think it makes sense that someone
somewhere is using
a washboard to mash grapes
for dying sheets
for putting on beds
to be slept in
by sexy naked big-dicked teenage boys?
why do sexy naked big-dicked teenage boys
need to sleep on sheets that have been
dyed with grape juice? and why must
those grapes have been mashed on
an old-fashioned washboard?
you think any of this makes sense?
that movie that you saw that
made 3 trillion dollars world-wide
is
just as good as
the one that sputtered
out in the first week,
and no one ever saw again,
until it achieved cult status, that
is, and went on to make
a respectable 8 trillion.
and that first movie,

the one that made 3 trillion,
falls into disfavor, and
when people see it at
drive-ins, they're only
interested in having
sex with the person
that they
brought to the drive-in
because they hoped
to have sex in the car with
that person. does it make
any sense that they go to
a movie and then don't watch it
at all? of course you could
say they just want the privacy
of being alone in a car
at a drive-in, and they got
taught that drive-ins are sexy
places to have sex,
and
when, in one of the cars, the
two sexy big-dicked teenage boys
who are in the front seat of that car
unzip each other's pants and
jerk each other off into their butter-drenched
popcorn napkins
during the most exciting part
of the movie, does it
make any sense that
the two sexy big-dicked teenage boys
use popcorn napkins
to catch their jets of cum? no,
not really, but kinda sorta.
listen, you just can't look
for the logic in certain things,
because there is none.
does it make sense that an
asteroid crashed into the earth
and killed all the dinosaurs?
does it make sense that
some people think

the earth is only 6 thousand years old?
when dinosaurs died out millions of
years ago?
summary:
"believing that stuff makes
sense,
just doesn't make sense,"
thinks the sexy naked big-dicked teenage boy
as he lies on his back alone atop his
bed in the middle of the night,
and tugs on his dick
and tugs on his dick
waiting the moment of orgasm
when the cum goes spurting out
of that tiny little pee hole at the
tip of his great-big dick,
and the origin of the universe
is jellied toast on the back
of a sea turtle,
mermaids singing lullabies
at the top of their lungs.

blowing out the candle

"the sky folded, and then split in two.
there were lots of flames in the split site.
like a zipper unzipped, and flames behind
the teeth of the zipper."
the good-looking sexy big-dicked teenage boy
was describing a recent dream he'd had.
the good-looking sexy big-dicked teenage boy
was saying these words to his psychologist.
his psychologist, a wise and, physically,
a very ugly man, but with a big
and beautiful heart,
said,
"so you clearly have feelings about
never having had sex before. is it flames
that you see waiting for you behind those labial lips
of a hot vagina?"
the good-looking sexy big-dicked teenage boy
cringed. "is it that obvious?" he asked.
"seems pretty damn obvious to me,"
said his psychologist.
then, almost inexplicably,
both the good-looking sexy big-dicked teenage boy
and his psychologist
chuckled. then, their chuckles broke into
warm friendly laughter.
they truly liked each other,
the good-looking sexy big-dicked teenage boy
and his psychologist,
and it
was a beautiful day
to talk, and swear, and
make peace out of anxiety,
sense out
of buffalo nickles,
all stacked up on top of each other,
leaning like the leaning tower of pisa,
or, jutting up,
like a penis.
"i suppose you'd really like

to get your virginity done and
over with,
wouldn't you?" said
his psychologist.
"yep," said the good-looking sexy big-dicked teenage boy.
"well," said his psychologist,
"let's talk about that some more, shall we?"
ah a nice day in that office, the walls
dark and varnished, and the smell of
furniture polish, quietly comforting.

green

cute boys who paint pictures with their dicks
are the bee's knees. cute boys who dip
the tips of their big dicks into paint,
and then paint pictures with their dicks,
are god's gift to the universe.
these cute boys work with big canvases,
mounted low on the easel.
their days are spent copious, surrounded
by beauty, enveloped in the scent
of their oily pubic hair.
sometimes these cute boys get so
excited while they are painting, their
dicks get so stiff, that their
hot freshly-spurted cum gets
mixed in with the paint on their
canvases, and dries there,
along with the paint. after
a day spent painting with
their dicks, the cute boys
who paint paintings with
their dicks settle into
a nice sudsy bath, and
try to get their hardworking
dicks clean, but, truth be
told, their dicks are
never really clean ever
again, but retain the
sheen, the tinge,
of rampant creativity.
as they get older,
these dyed-dick
boys never think of
themselves as tainted, or dirty,
but just, perhaps,
as gently used.

birthstone

he liked his boys naked, on the couch, crawling all over
each other. not that he wanted them doing sexual
things with each other -- he didn't really want to
see that, but, if one of them happened to sprout
a hardon while they were bouncing around together on
the couch, that was fine with him. he just liked
to see them happy, jostling all around together,
one big crawly bouncy-bouncy fest of tight
young skin and sweet handsome faces.
**
mostly, they came from the local
university, and from the local high
school. they just kind of showed
up, magically. first they weren't
there. then they were.
**
one afternoon, when it was
nice and sunny and the sunlight
was streaming in through the
living room window,
his boys were naked,
bouncing around on the couch,
crawling all over each other.
they were telling jokes and
laughing. one of them had
a hardon.
**
he liked
that, all of his boys
being on the couch that way.
he liked everything about it.
**
when the boy with the
hardon got a little too
excited and started spurting
cum, all the other boys
sprouted hardons, too.
things kinda went
a bit crazy after that.

it was almost more than
he could stand.
he could barely look
at them to see what
would happen next.
**

after a while, though,
his boys were once again
bouncing around naked
on the couch, telling
jokes, the sunlight streaming
in. once again the illusion of tranquility
sustained him. there in that peaceable
kingdom, there in his
little house
by the sea.

pony farm

the splish splash i'm taking a bath
sounds
being made by the sexy naked big-dicked teenage boy
long about saturday night
were splishy and splashy and wet and soapy
and squeezy turgid dick
flopping around on top of the water
almost ready to spurt cum
and
the sexy naked big-dicked teenage boy
wonders if he's going to spurt his cum
right into his own face
and then wash the cum off his face
or if he's going to submerge his
big hard dick right before
the moment he cums
and thus spurt his cum into the hot soapy water
jostling for position
his dick above the water
his dick below the water
sliding his tight firm butt around
on the bottom of the slick hot tub
his dick out of the water
his dick under the water
splishing and splashing
and taking a bath
long about saturday night
and
when
the sexy naked big-dicked teenage boy
cums
his dick is out of the water
and his cum
spurts out and hits
him right on the lips
and on his forehead
and some of it goes right
over his head and hits
the back of the tub

the sexy naked big-dicked teenage boy
spurting cum
splishing and
splashing
long about
saturday night.
the cum on his
face, he scrunches
under the water
and rubs his hands
over his face
and around his
chin
and touches his
adam's apple,
there under the soapy
water,
the sexy naked big-dicked teenage boy
groans and growls
mouthing out bubbles
under
the water
and then
he sticks his
face out of the water
and grins
like a hot sexy maniac
who's just had a whole lota
fun spurting cum
splishing and splashing
and taking a bath
long about saturday
night.

alive

people have wondered about Frankenstein's dick.
not the Dr. but the Monster.
people have been asking questions about Frankenstein's dick.
people want to know.
people wish Mary Godwin Wollstonecraft Shelley (wife of
Percy Bysshe Shelley) had told them.
about the dick.
about Frankenstein's dick.
people wish she'd have made the story sexier.
people have been clamoring.
forming little garrulous knots and murmuring.
"i wish she'd have told us about Frankenstein's dick" they say.
"i wish she'd have told us."
lying naked on the table, the fully assembled monster had a
big big big big big male member.
she might have said.
the phallus swelled and lifted its phallic head as the rich dark
blood began to circulate through the monster's body.
she might have said.
the first thing the jolt of electricity effected
was the instant turgidity in the monster's male part that caused
it to come to life and
spurt
its white manly liquid instantaneously and copiously, and
fill the room with the scent of tall muscular maleness in all its
musky earthy
overripeness.
she might have said.
but she didn't.
and people have wondered about Frankenstein's dick ever since.
little mumbles of curiosity.
little whimpers of prurient interest.
little shouts and pants and moans
from under their sheets
in thick summer nights.

the dewberry capital of america

almost nobody eats dewberries
anymore.
in fact, hardly anyone
has heard of them.
but there's a town in
north carolina that
grew rich off
dewberries. but
that happened
many years ago.
that town
still exists though,
a shadow of
its former self
as the saying
goes -- and
as the flies began gathering on the rotting dewberries,
the remains of the town sank into a chaos of antique stores
and tasty little cafes, the bamboo shoots shot up
100 feet, and the water tower rusted to a shade
of tawny blotchy brown. oh what a town it
had once been though, the pies and cakes
and tasty cookies, the envy of all those
all around, who came to soak up the goodies.
**
out in the old dewberry beds,
the sexy young men slunk into the
heart of the thorns, eyed each other
naked, and took action to commence
the spurting of cum--never took
very long, and after, the smoking
of cigarettes and the sipping
of advanced quality beer and ale,
the bluebirds cheerful as always,
as they sought solace in
the fronds of the ferns,
lapping at the edges
of where wonderous harvests
had once occurred. now, nobody

has even heard of a dewberry
anymore. things that were
once popular, no longer
are.
**
the sexy naked young men
slink from their hiding place
in the old dewberry beds,
go down to the river,
wash themselves nearly
clean. the hint
of lust hangs about
their ears, though,
and their scrotal sacs as well,
their fingertips
still delicate from
the ghostly antique blue.

the rewards of subtlety

sitting in the sauna there
in the men's
locker room of his
college's gymnasium,
the sexy big-dicked sophomore
is naked, but with his towel
draped loosely around his waist.
**
he's waiting for,
hoping for,
someone, anyone
hopeful, to join
him in the sauna.
**
he's still alone, though,
and
when he
gets a hardon,
the tip of his
dick is exposed, and pokes out
from between the parted halves of
his towel. alas,
he's still the only one in
the sauna, so much for
dreams of seduction, water
smell the soap
of merciless
shampoo. when he spurts
cum, the
chessboard goes back to
truce, no battles, no messy
skirmishes between the
knights.

better pounce on it

when climbing the mountains with goats,
expect to wake from your dream
with the scent of musk clinging to
your pubic hair, the oily hair
of nannies and billies
having left a bit of residue
behind on your skin,
your fingertips,
your flared-out protesting nostrils.
you will not like these
smells clinging to you,
and the scent of
goats high in the mountains
was much more goat, and
much less mountain,
than you'd expected.
**
as the cattle cross the
road deep in the country,
and you sit there waiting
for them to hurry
up and get across, you
ask yourself why
you went for this drive
in the country in the
first place. you're in
unfamiliar territory here.
perhaps you're even lost.
the cattle take
their time, and
when finally a farmer
at the end of the line
shoos the last cow
on across, and waves
a friendly enough little
wave at you,
you are so glad
to be on your way,
that you almost

forget where you're
on your way back to.
**
later that night, sitting
down to dinner with your family,
you suddenly want to
see your
sexy teenage son completely naked,
and are almost about to
suggest that he take off his clothes,
then and there, and
show you, and everyone there,
what is surely his great big smooth
dick,
when
you stop those words,
and fill your mouth with
mashed potatoes, instead.
everyone looks at you a bit
funny,
and no, it's not just
your imagination.
**
adrift, the sky down
below you is filled with
birds -- crows, and sparrows,
and every size in between.
it's peaceful here.
you want to stay.

plasma pilfering

zee-zuu
i am in my prime.
i am 27 years old
i am lean lithe athletic
my muscles are rippling
my shirt is off
i am sawing down a tree
that is blocking the view of
the mountains from the
back of our house
zee-zuu zee-zuu zee-zuu
the sound of my little
cross-cut saw as i saw
down a gigantic tulip poplar.
this is a big tree.
if it falls the wrong way,
it could fall on our house.
i am young, daring, foolish,
sexy. my shirt is off
zee-zuu zee-zuu zee-zuu
the sound of my little saw
as i saw on that big
ole tree
my shirt off
my muscles rippling
sexy me as i
zee-zuu zee-zuu zee-zuu
and when the tree finally
falls, it falls in
the right direction
it doesn't hit the house
it falls down the mountain
just like i wanted
it to.
i go inside
strip off the few
clothes i'm wearing
masturbate in the shower
i feel good

really really
good
**

and now i'm 62 years old
no longer 27
no longer lean lithe athletic
no longer in the woods
suburbanized now
and just getting
older.
**

zee-zuu zee-zuu zee-zuu
hasn't anybody ever
heard a cross-cut saw, and
doesn't it really
make that sound?

triton the magnificent

the sexy young man has spent the
day with his friends. they are
all inside now, and he is
out here in his own back yard,
all alone. it is a hot summer evening.
now, while he's out here in
his back yard,
his friends are inside his house,
drinking beer and watching television.
and, for this moment,
he's here, alone in the back yard,
drinking beer from a
sweaty brown bottle.
he's felt lonely before,
but nothing like this,
as the evening falls,
and
the first goddamn star
peeks out like
a silver button,
on a lost coat,
that he wore in
the winter,
on the coldest
day of them all.

the good ship lollipop

dead pigs are certainly tasty, aren't
they? except you're not supposed
to say you're eating a dead pig.
you're supposed to call it "ham" or
"pork". even though everyone
knows it's a dead pig:
spices up the nose,
and perhaps a hot dog up its
pink little piggy ass.
"if you think some of the boys in
LORD OF THE FLIES didn't
fuck some of the other boys
up their tight little asses,
well then,
you've just got no understanding
of great literature,"
thinks
the sexy naked big-dicked teenage boy
as
he watches himself jerk off
in front of the bathroom
mirror --
habits are such hard things
to break.

the invincibility clause

when i was a college sophomore,
i sometimes used to
jerk off in
the empty
football stadium at night.
i'd take off all
my clothes
and spurt my
cum
onto the short smooth
incredibily well-manicured grass.
then i'd get dressed and
climb the fence designed to
protect the college football stadium
from people such as me.
and then as i
walked back to
my dorm
i'd wonder
why, precisely, i do
this kind of thing,
and try to figure out exactly how
many times i've done it, how long this
has been going on, and
how long until i get
caught at it,
which seems like never-never land,
in the big field
of ain't never gonna happen
but if it did happen
if i did get caught
who would be the
one who found me
and then what
would happen next?
would it be sexy
or horrible
or just

horribly sexy?
i get back to the dorm and go on
inside. it is quite late.
i hum an odd little tune
as i climb into bed.
my roommate says "shut the hell up."
i say "fuck you."
and that, as they say, is
that.

Acknowledgements:

The author gratefully acknowledges the following publications where some of these poems first appeared: *BareBack Magazine*, *Chiron Review*, *The Commonline Journal*, *FUCK!*, *My Favorite Bullet*, and *Nerve Cowboy*.

The author would also like to thank BareBack Editor/Publisher Peter Jelen for always treating me and my poems so nice. Thanks, Pete! You're a sweet gentle wild man, and it's great working with you.

About the Author:

Carl Miller Daniels lives in the United States. He's not a cowboy, but thinks about them a lot. His poems have appeared in many nice places, including *Assaracus, BareBack Magazine, Chiron Review, Citizens for Decent Literature, The Commonline Journal, DNA Magazine, FUCK!, My Favorite Bullet,* and *Zygote in my Coffee*. Daniels has three other chapbooks in print. His first full-length book, *Gorilla Architecture*, was published by Interior Noise Press. His full-length follow up, *Saline*, was published in November 2014, also by Interior Noise Press. Daniels and his partner, Jon (aka "the sweetest man in the world"), have lived together for over 30 years.

Also by the Author

Museum Quality Orgasm

Riot Act

Shy Boys at Home

Gorilla Architecture

Saline

www.ingramcontent.com/pod-product-compliance
Lightning Source LLC
Chambersburg PA
CBHW061344040426
42444CB00011B/3082